Spend Wisely

BY HEATHER E. SCHWARTZ

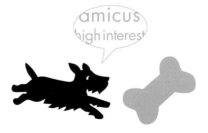

amicus
high interest

Amicus High Interest is published by Amicus
P.O. Box 1329, Mankato, MN 56002
www.amicuspublishing.us

Library of Congress Cataloging-in-Publication Data
Schwartz, Heather E.
 Spend wisely / by Heather E. Schwartz.
    pages cm. – (Money smarts)
Includes bibliographical references and index.
Audience: K to Grade 3.
Summary: "This photo-illustrated book for elementary readers helps readers learn the basics of wants and needs, shopping sales, and making wise purchases. Gives tips on saving money for big purchases and finding the best prices"– Provided by publisher.
ISBN 978-1-60753-795-3 (library binding)
ISBN 978-1-60753-904-9 (ebook)
1. Shopping–Juvenile literature. 2. Consumer education–Juvenile literature. I. Title.
 TX335.5.S393 2015
 640.73–dc23

                          2014037649

Editor: Wendy Dieker
Series Designer: Kathleen Petelinsek
Book Designer: Aubrey Harper
Photo Researcher: Derek Brown

Photo Credits: 237/Paul Bradbury/Ocean/Corbis cover, JGI/Jamie Grill/Blend Images/Corbis 5, Sean Justice/Corbis 6, B. Leighty/Photri Images/Alamy 9, JGI/Jamie Grill/Blend Images/Corbis 10-11, Andrew Melbourne/Alamy 13, Zero Creatives/Corbis 14, jf/cultura/Corbis 16-17, zhu difeng/Shutterstock 18, KidStock/Blend Images/Corbis 21, David Sacks/Getty 22, Keith Seaman - Camerad Inc/Getty 25, Geri Lavrov/Getty 26, BJI/Blue Jean Images/Getty 29

Printed in Malaysia.

10 9 8 7 6 5 4 3 2 1

Table of Contents

Why Spend Wisely?

Do you get a weekly allowance? Do relatives give you cash on your birthday? When you have money, you probably want to spend it. But don't run out to the store just yet. You can't buy everything you want. You'll run out of money. You need to spend wisely.

It is great to get money. How can you spend it wisely?

Save money in a piggy bank until you decide how to spend it.

When you have money, you have three choices: save, share, or spend. Saving your money means you will have money in the future. Sharing your money with people in need is a good way to help them. But when you spend money, you have to decide which things are best to buy.

Needs and Wants

How can you spend wisely? First figure out what you need. **Needs** are the basics. We all need a home and clothing. We would die without food and water.

But some needs are more than basics. You could live without pencils. But you need them at school. If you play softball, you need a glove. Spending on needs is spending wisely.

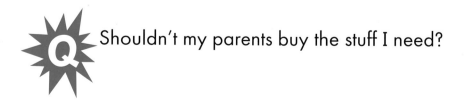 Shouldn't my parents buy the stuff I need?

Softball players might need to buy a uniform, shoes, and a glove.

Your parents probably buy plenty of your needs. But some kids buy their own school supplies or clothes.

Wants are items that we don't need to survive. Wants are often fun things like new games or treats. If you spend all your money on wants, you won't have enough for your needs.

Sometimes it's hard to tell which is which. Potato chips and candy are food. But are they needs? No. They are junk foods. You can live without them.

Donuts are a treat. You don't need them to live.

Sometimes an item we need can be a want too. Let's say you need a hat. You could get a plain black hat. Or you could get one with your favorite sports team on it. That one is more **expensive**. You need a hat to keep warm. But you don't need one that costs lots of money.

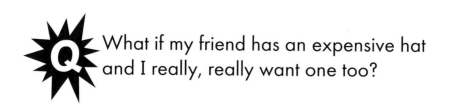 What if my friend has an expensive hat and I really, really want one too?

Hats come in all styles and all prices! How much is a hat worth to you?

 Think hard about why you want the expensive hat. If it's only because your friend has it, you probably do not need it.

Wise shoppers plan how they will spend their money.

Making a Plan

Before you shop, decide what you want to buy. Make a list. Maybe you need a new backpack and a gift for your sister. You also want a new toy.

At the store, you will have more choices. You might not have enough money for everything on your list. You will have to choose. Which things are the most important?

When you get to the store, you might see something else. Sunglasses! If you buy something that's not on your list, it's an **impulse purchase**. Stick to the items on your list for today. Put the glasses on a list for another day. Save up some money for them. If you still want the sunglasses when you have enough money, buy them then.

Don't get distracted by items that you don't need to buy today.

16

Wise spenders buy things on sale.
They try not to pay full price.

Getting a Good Deal

Smart shoppers find the best price. Suppose you want to buy a video game. The game you want costs $35. You might be able to find a lower price. You can watch for a **sale**. You could look for **coupons**. Then you can get the game for a lower price. You'll have to wait, but it is wise to spend less.

Not all stores sell things for the same price. Look in other stores. You might find the game for a lower price somewhere else. Ask your parents if you can look online. But watch out for shipping costs. The game might cost $30 online, but it might cost $10 to ship it. You'll pay a total of $40. The store price of $35 is cheaper.

These boys are looking online for a good price on a game they want.

You might find a good
price at a yard sale.

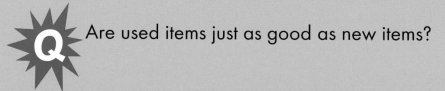 Are used items just as good as new items?

Let's say you've been to all the stores. You looked online. But you still haven't found a low price. What now? Consider looking for used items. A **consignment shop** sells things someone else owned. You will usually find a lower price. Check out yard sales and flea markets too.

 Sometimes. Check over the item and try it out before you buy it.

Beware of deals that don't really help you save. You might find a deal that gives you a second item at half price. For example, if you buy a lunchbox for $10, you can buy another for $5. The price sounds right. But if you won't use the second lunchbox, it's just a waste of money.

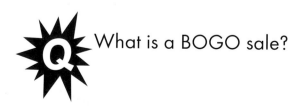
Q What is a BOGO sale?

If you only need one lunchbox, a deal to get two lunchboxes might be a waste.

 BOGO means Buy One, Get One. It can be a good deal if you need two of the item.

You might want to buy expensive markers if they will work much better than cheaper ones.

Q What if something I buy doesn't work at all?

Spending Smart

Price isn't the only thing that matters when you shop. **Quality** counts, too. In some cases, paying more means getting a better product. Suppose you want to buy new markers. One set costs $10. Another costs $1. Be careful of a price that's very low. The cheap markers may not last very long or work very well.

 Always keep your **receipt**. If something doesn't work, take it back to the store. Ask for a new one or your money back.

Wise spenders also know to buy just the things they need. Let's say you find an art kit filled with supplies. But you really only need paper. It's better to save your money and just buy paper.

When you make smart choices, you won't waste money. Smart spenders buy important things first. They are happy with what they buy.

This boy found a good price on a shirt. How will you spend wisely?

Glossary

consignment shop A store that sells used items.

coupon A slip of paper that allows the person who has it to get a lower price at the store.

expensive Costing a lot of money.

impulse purchase An item that was bought without planning.

needs Things that you need to live, such as food and water; needs can also be things you need for activities or school.

quality How well-made something is; good quality items are well-made and will last a long time.

receipt A slip of paper that shows what you bought and how much you paid for it.

sale When a store lowers a price on things they sell.

wants Things that are fun to have, but not things you need to live; toys, games, and candy are often considered wants.

Read More

Furgang, Kathy. *National Geographic Kids Everything Money.* Washington, D.C.: National Geographic Children's Books, 2013.

Larson, Jennifer S. *What Can You Do With Money? Earning, Spending, and Saving.* Minneapolis, Minnesota: Lerner Publishing Group, 2010.

Rau, Dana Meachen. *Spending Money.* New York, New York: Gareth Stevens Publishing, 2010.

Websites

The Mint: Spending
www.themint.org/kids/spending.html

PBS Kids: Mad Money
pbskids.org/itsmylife/games/mad_money_flash.html

PBS Kids: Spending Smarts: Think Before You Buy!
pbskids.org/itsmylife/money/spendingsmarts/

Index

About the Author

Heather E. Schwartz has written books for young readers on all kinds of topics. She was excited to write about money because it can be earned and used in so many interesting ways. She recently spent some savings on a fun purchase: two kittens! Visit Heather's website at www.heathereschwartz.com.